The
AUTHORITY
and
INTERPRETATION
of
SCRIPTURE

A Statement of
The United Church of Canada

THE UNITED CHURCH PUBLISHING HOUSE

Grateful acknowledgement is made for permission to reprint from copyrighted material, including the following:

From *What Bible Are Your Children Reading?* by William H. Willimon. Copyright © 1991 Christian Century Foundation. Reprinted by permission from the July 24-31, 1991 issue of *The Christian Century*.

Canadian Cataloguing in Publication Data

United Church of Canada
    The authority and interpretation of Scripture

Prepared by the Theology and Faith Committee for the General Council of the United Church of Canada.
Includes bibliographical references.
ISBN 1-55134-002-X

1. Bible - Evidences, authority, etc. 2. Bible - Criticism, interpretation, etc. 3. Bible - Use. 4. United Church of Canada - Doctrines. I. United Church of Canada. Theology and Faith Committee. II. Title.

BS480.U65 1992   220.1'3   C92-095113-9

The United Church Publishing House
85 St. Clair Avenue East
Toronto, Ontario
M4T 1M8

Printed in Canada by Hignell Printing Limited.

CONTENTS

PREFACE

The following motion was passed at the 34th General Council of The United Church of Canada:

1) THAT General Council receive the document.

2) THAT General Council endorse the following standards of evaluation for any claim to authority in the life and work of The United Church of Canada:
   — God's historic self-revelation in Jesus Christ is crucial in establishing what has legitimate authority in Christian community.
   — Legitimate authority, in every case, enhances community of the whole created earth.
   — The Word of God, in every case, is larger than the text of the Bible.

3) THAT, in the light of these standards, General Council endorse the following Convictions:
   — God calls us to engage the Bible as foundational authority as we seek to live the Christian life.
   — God calls us to engage the Bible as a church seeking God's community with all people, living creatures, and the earth.
   — God calls us to engage the Bible to experience the liberating and transforming Word of God.
   — God calls us to engage the Bible with an awareness of our

theological, social, and cultural assumptions.

— God calls us to engage the Bible with a sense of sacred mystery and in dynamic interaction with human experience, understanding, and heritage.

— God calls us to engage the Bible trusting God's Spirit to enliven our understanding and to empower our acting.

4) THAT General Council Divisions integrate these standards and convictions into all aspects of their life and work, and that Conferences, Presbyteries, and Pastoral Charges be encourged to do the same.

5) THAT General Council respond to the many voices in the church requesting opportunities and resources for biblical study.

   a) By encouraging ministerial leadership to:

      i) take the risk of making the resources of biblical scholarship accessible to congregations, through sermons, Christian education programmes for persons of all ages, and such other means as seem necessary;

      ii) learn how to educate about the Bible;

   b) By encouraging congregations to accept that engaging the Bible is not optional for the Christian community and challenging them to take the risk of such engagement.

   c) By requesting that the Division of Mission in Canada assist in that process.

6) THAT the 34th General Council make a gift of the following insights to the congregations:

   — Engaging the Bible is not optional for the Christian community.

— When we engage the Bible, individually and collectively, we are deeply influenced by and entangled in the world-views of the particular nation/community/family in which we live.

— Our interpretation of scripture is most clearly shown in the way we live.

— Interpretation is unavoidable when we are engaging the Bible.

— Each interpretation is an invitation to ever new discoveries and insights into God's convenant with life and the earth.

And, THAT congregations be encouraged to continue to share their insights arising out of their own biblical study with the Theology and Faith Committee.

34th General Council
Fredericton, N.B.
August 1992

I

INTRODUCTION

From October 1989 to the end of 1990, the United Church was involved in the study of the document *The Authority and Interpretation of Scripture* (referred to as the Study Document in this report). As the statistics show, in terms of the sheer number of persons involved and responses received, it has been one of the most extensive church studies. People came to the study with different levels of energy and spiritual expressions and with a variety of expectations and assumptions. A participant in one conference event spoke for many involved in the study when she said, "People came ... looking for a garden ready to harvest but were given dirt and tools." It is a good metaphorical description; what we offer as a report reflects the labour of many Christian people, at home and abroad, who were not afraid to plow in with hope of a good harvest.

As we offer the produce of that harvest, the question arises: why did we plant the garden in the first place?

As early as 1985, the General Council Executive gave some

urgency to the task of clarifying the United Church's position on scripture. It requested the Theology and Faith Committee to assume leadership in this regard. In response, the committee brought a report on scripture to the 32nd General Council. It was received and the following motion was passed:

> *That the General Council receive this document and*
> *commend it to the church for reflection and response*
> *with a report to the 33rd General Council.*

A second motion was passed, in the context of debate on the report "Toward a Christian Understanding of Sexual Orientation, Lifestyles and Ministry," expanding the terms of the first motion. It read:

> *That there be further church-wide study of the authority*
> *and interpretation of scripture and the theological and*
> *cultural premises that inform our understanding.*

Such references encourage us to question more deeply. Why such a mandate? A number of reasons may be given. The church sensed among its members a desire to have their voices and views on scripture heard. In addition, it recognized that the nature of authority was unclear for many in the church in a way that affected every area of life. The church realized that few things are accepted on face value anymore — even the Bible. Some assumptions about the Bible's place and significance in our lives, individually and collectively, were being questioned. It was becoming clear that few Christians (including United Church members) regularly read or study the Bible and that answers to perplexing moral and ethical questions could not immediately be drawn from its pages. What authority, then, does it have with us and how does that authority arise for us? Those were the substantive questions resting at the heart of the study as a whole. General Council carries the belief that our faith life as a community will be helpfully defined and thereby strengthened by attending to these questions. The Theology and Faith Committee, in keeping with its mandate (study, clarify, and make provision for the issuance of position statements), prepared resources and initiated a church-wide study process, seeking to establish convictions for the use and place of scripture in our life as a church.

We believe that the manner in which the members of committee attempted to fulfill their role is significant. We began in 1988 by preparing a text for discussion and response. It represented a position on the topic intended to promote dialogue between church members and the committee, and between our church and other denominations. It was written to invite people to reflect on their own experiences, and, in that light, to share their own convictions. The nature of the document was thus conversational and not dogmatic. The Study Document was never intended to be a theo-logical declaration, decree, or an external authority over the church. It was intended to be a tool for promoting conversation within the church, with the hope of developing convictions for engaging the Bible.[1] Trusting in the power of God's Spirit, we expected, as a committee, that the dialogue between the Study Document as "text" and the reader would bring new insight and understanding. We believe this has happened, and we have tried to express our insights in this report.

At every step of the study process, there was a high level of participation by people in different groups and settings. In the preparation of the study document itself, specific congregations and individuals were invited to offer criticism and suggestions for

1.   See part 3, "Convictions," 27.

its revision. In the actual study of the document more than 1,200 responses were received from Sessions, groups, individuals and partner churches. A very significant consultation was held in Brazil in March 1990, hosted by our partner church, The Methodist Church of Brazil. We are indebted to the Division of World Outreach for their leadership in setting up this forum. In May 1991, eleven conference events, in conjunction with the Annual Conference meetings, were held for the purpose of testing the directions and convictions emerging from the study at that point. These were well attended and extremely beneficial in the preparation of the report. Again, we are indebted to the work of conference staff persons and presbytery liaison persons for creating these opportunities. Most presbyteries responded to our initial request to have key contact facilitators of the study appointed and they were a valuable re-source to the committee, alert, challenging, affirming, and faithful to the task at hand.

It has been said that a camel is a horse prepared by a committee. Some people, in reading our report, may wish to describe it in camel-like terms. The report does not have the touch of a single writer, but of several, as the different styles reveal. Nevertheless, it was received, worked on, and adopted as a whole by the Theology and Faith Committee. We acknowledge with gratitude the editorial work of Michael Webster and the administrative assistance of Susan Simms, Caryn Douglas, Jody Abernethy, and Mary Purdon. We also acknowledge the contribution of former members of the Theology and Faith Committee from 1985 to 1990: Stan MacKay, Dee McEachern, Genevieve Carder, Joan McMurty, David Newman, Gerald Hopkirk, James Pan, and Gordon Daly.

Although the work seemed endless and even burdensome at times, as a committee we were grateful for the chance to be in conversation with the whole church on a matter of such theological and practical importance. For many, the study and the questions pursuant to it were difficult, for they created painful uncertainties and ambiguities in an area of life where they are least desired or accepted. As a result, this study has been an exercise in theology and emotion. A refreshing delight, however, was that people, in responding, were not afraid to risk the expressions of both. Out of that richness of faith and life has come a theological offering which we hope will be seen and received as worthy, given the value of our heritage, the importance of people's present experiences, and the mission of the gospel to which the scriptures themselves bear witness and to which we are called.

Theology and Faith Committee
Robert Anderson, Ross Bartlett, Gwyn Griffith, Janice Guthrie, Richard Hollingsworth, Mary Jane Hudgins, Marilyn Legge, Hallett Llewellyn (Staff), David MacLachlan (Chair), Margaret MacPherson, Greer Anne Ng, John Young.

II

CHURCH AND SOCIETAL CONTEXT
OF OUR REPORT

Why Context?

We do most of our work within a specific context. Our life as The
United Church of Canada — as congregations, committees,
presbyteries, conferences, and the General Council — takes place
within a certain context in our life and our world. We have always
sought to be deeply engaged with the realities of God's world and
the people and institutions in it. Sometimes we have led the world
and framed new issues, sometimes we have followed and responded. We have not always been good at stating explicitly the
context in which we have been working. Repeatedly, responses to
the Study Document have indicated that context is crucially important for people as they seek to engage the Bible in a faithful manner.
The strongest expression was that of a Brazilian lay worker. Speaking of people who do not consider context when they read the Bible,
he said that their faith was "unglued from reality."

Concern for context is also found in the Bible. Before they ever became the scriptures of the wider community, the books of the Bible were written to and for a specific group or individual. Generally, when we engage the Bible and, in turn, find it engaging our lives, it is because it is addressing a specific issue, concern, or question. We address questions to the Bible. Some of those same questions were asked by readers of the Study Document: Why was it written? What prompted the authors to take certain positions? What were we seeking to accomplish? These questions were raised, both by those who were seeking to enter into serious dialogue with the committee and by those who saw hidden motives behind every word! In this report we hope to demonstrate that we have learned from those who asked us to pay more attention to context.

THE CONTEXT IN 1988-92

The United Church of Canada

The initial report on this subject by our committee to the 1988 General Council went largely unnoticed by a church and Council absorbed with the painful questions of sexual orientation and ministry. Since Victoria, the church has been variously described as "touchy," "wounded," "recovering," "moving on to other matters." It has been a time of difficult decision making and adjustment for many people. Some had looked to the Study Document for a response to "Membership, Ministry and Human Sexuality." That was never the intention of the committee or the General Council. Nevertheless, that expectation formed part of the context in which the study document was received or rejected, ignored or studied. There were other expressions of this general malaise in the church at large. Most of those comments indicated that the church felt

7

"studied out" after dealing with a large number of difficult issues in recent years. As well, many people were averse to dealing with any issue that might be perceived as controversial. Significant cynicism exists in some congregations regarding the structures of the church and the impact of the "grass roots" on the decisions of the General Council and its committees. In contrast, we found large numbers of people prepared to invest vast amounts of time in study and reflection on this subject. As a committee, we are both overwhelmed and humbled by the enthusiastic response people have given to the study. We received hundreds of comments, including many from those most critical of the process, that show deep reflection and a careful crafting of responses. It seems the people of the United Church have a reservoir of concern and commitment that they are prepared to tap for issues that touch them. This willingness illustrates something important emerging in The United Church of Canada. Our developing practice is to deal with issues by asking people what they think and believe, and then taking seriously what they say.

In recent years many people have felt compelled to examine the Bible and their own faith. Many grasped with eagerness the limited tools that the Study Document (which was never intended to be a Bible study programme) afforded them. There was a strong sense that the Study Document, which encouraged conversation about different understandings of scripture passages, allowed for some mutual understanding of difficulties and formed the basis for some degree of healing. Some discovered (or rediscovered) the Bible's crucial role, not as a weapon against others, but as a means of discovering God's judgment and grace for ourselves. All these factors, to one degree or another, formed the context in which the Study Document was addressed (or ignored) by various communities within the church.

Another contextual factor facing the study and this report is an awareness of the increasing marginalization of the church in Canadian society. It is hard for us to describe this reality completely because we are in the midst of the change. Many people resist the recognition that the church is no longer at the centre of our society. Ever-shrinking budgets in every aspect of church life and work, the increasing pluralization of Canadian society, a growing awareness that not everyone wants to be "just like us" — all indicate the changing place of the mainline Christian denominations in our nation. Some in the church decry these changes as a sign of the faithlessness and apostasy of our nation. Others see this as an opportunity to return to the perceived purity and faithfulness of the early church. For the majority, however, the changes have yet to be sorted and integrated into a clear and coherent vision.

The National and International Context

Our national and international context is constantly changing. We can point to some parts of the context in which the Study Document was discussed and invite readers to reflect on their present context.

As Canadians, we are learning in a new way that the patience of many of our Native sisters and brothers is running out, as they seek a just and lasting solution to their grievances. The violent confrontations at Kanawake and Kanasatake, the decisions against the Temagami band claim and that of the Gitksan-Wet'suwet'en, the provincial commissions acknowledging that the justice system is not always adequate or just for Native Canadians, and the inclusion of Native leaders in the deliberations of the premiers are all signs that a new shape is emerging in the relations between the First Nations and the dominant culture. We have also seen the racial tensions that exist below the appearance of a calm and harmonious social surface. This intolerance has also been brought to light by several federal and provincial inquiries into Canada's future. We have learned that Canada is far more peaceful and just for some than for others.

A series of international events has touched us during the lifetime of the Study Document. These events have had domestic ramifications. The euphoria over major changes in Eastern Europe, the latest Russian revolution, and the effective end of the Cold War has been tempered by the realization that a new integration of Europe has resulted in profound dislocation and hardship for many. Global economic recession has manifested in Canada in the permanent loss of many manufacturing jobs, agricultural subsidy wars, disruption in the fishing industry on both coasts, greater poverty, heavier demands on welfare and food banks, and increased homelessness. In response, many governmental and social agencies have limited those programmes that aid those who form the largest part of the underclass: women, youth, minorities, the handicapped. The conflict in the Persian Gulf and the resultant tragedy of the Kurdish people again focused our awareness on how easily we turn to violent, technological solutions to differences. Tragically, we cannot muster even a fraction of those resources to meet genuine human suffering. The Gulf War also revealed our genuine ambivalence about the use of outdated and violent methods to preserve a world order benefiting a privileged few. In turn, we witnessed deep-seated suspicion of the glib and sanitized reporting of mass destruction. Since the London General Council (1990), our church's attention and awareness of environmental issues and opportunities (e.g., James Bay II) has increased dramatically, a development paralleled across the nation. All of these national and international concerns have been reflected in (sometimes acrimonious) discussions within the church. The apparent general lack of confidence in traditional solutions for any of these questions is worth noting.

As we try to name our context more explicitly, we must also consider with great seriousness the role and place of community. A "community" is a social location. Most of us are part of a number of communities—work, school, family, church, neighbourhoods. As we listened to those who responded to the Study Document, we heard many affirm that it is within these communities that they most faithfully engage and respond to God's word. We need to be aware, however, that "community" is not without its negative aspects. Community is not always life-giving. The way one group of people creates its community can lead to exclusion and even death for others. As well as being life-giving, nurturing, and challenging, communities can be death-embracing, stifling, and demonic. God's word calls us to evaluate our communities in light of the qualities of God's eternal *shalom*. We recognize that some of our communities, including The United Church of Canada, have fostered racism and the marginalization of certain groups. As a church of power, the United Church has not always been faithful in nurturing life wherever it is found. As we move towards the margins of society and experience the loss of much of our prior influence, we are challenged to work towards greater and more empowering community for all. We must also acknowledge the fact that to speak of "community" may exclude those who feel they have no community. If we take Jesus as mentor and friend, we must seek ever more faithfully to include others, even as he reached out to include all.

AUTHORITY

Many of the domestic and global concerns noted above have revealed a deep and profound ambiguity regarding the nature and exercise of authority. Public opinion pollsters refer to this as "cynicism" regarding elected and appointed leaders. Our conviction is that it reflects a deep questioning of the use and nature of authority in many areas of society, including the life of the church.

A common observation regarding the Study Document was that it did not provide a definition of "authority." We took this observation seriously. We believe that definitions of authority, particularly in relation to the Bible, are most meaningfully understood as they are lived out in real life. Some people believe the Bible to be "the clear word of God," which should be followed literally. For others, the message of the Bible is much more ambiguous. How do we react when our society, upbringing, and inner desires indicate one course of action and our understanding of the "word of God" reveals another? How do we react when our sense of justice contradicts a scriptural text? Consider the issue of slavery. In the biblical text, slavery is condoned; yet slavery is opposed by Christians on the basis of the "sense of scripture" or the "call of Jesus." In such a situation, it is clear that the authority of scripture is not simply found in the written words of the text. It is only as we resolve these dilemmas that we begin to understand the authority of scripture, either for an individual or a community. Authority is found in the living interaction between the written text of the Bible and the lives of believers, as they are enlightened and empowered by the Spirit. We engage the text to encounter the Living Word.

Authority is a complex issue. It is not only exercised; we must also respond to it. Authority is intimately related to power. The issue in authority is how power is used. Furthermore, our understanding of the meaning of authority is related to our world-view. For example, *Webster's Dictionary* , reflecting one world-view, defines authority as the "power, because of rank or office, to give commands, enforce obedience, make decisions, etc." "Authority" in this view is expressed as "power over." There are, however, other world-views. The root of the word "authority" is the same as that of "author," and implies creativity, initiation, or the beginning of something new. Authority in this understanding comes from within the individual or community and is less precisely defined. "Authority" in this world-view can be expressed as "power with."

For much of history, authority was perceived to result from rank or office, with a few having power over many. With the Enlightenment of the eighteenth century, people were increasingly ready to challenge this notion. Today, more and more people are unwilling to believe that meaning is found entirely outside themselves. Increasingly, individuals and communities want to be involved in decisions that affect them and are reluctant to grant authority and power to a figure or institution "on high." Authority is being challenged when people find that its effects are not humanizing or liberating and freeing for significant groups. This challenging has led to a questioning of traditional authority in all areas of life, including the authority of the Bible as it has often been understood.

This questioning of authority in society as a whole is paralleled in many areas of our church's life. The United Church has a conciliar form of organization, which reflects a certain style of exercising authority. By "conciliar" we mean a series of courts (sessions, etc., presbyteries, conferences, General Council), each of which exercise responsibility for certain areas of the church's life and converse on areas held in common. Many people in congregations, however, are claiming that "the church" is not willing to listen. Others define the problem as a failure by some to understand the meaning and practice of such a system.

TYPES OF AUTHORITY

What is the relationship of authority to the individual? Is authority always external? Is it always a matter of others exercising authority over me? Are there occasions when I exercise authority in relation to my own life? Where is authority shared in community? Is it only when I give up certain things in order to enhance the life of the community? Or do the communities of which I am a part have an authority quite apart from anything I might relinquish to them? Or is this traditional way of talking about authority entirely inappropriate? The questions that we ask and the responses that we make reveal our view of authority.

If we ask, "Who's in charge?" or "What does it say in the book?", then we are saying that authority is external and that something outside of us has power over us. We have given power to another. We are looking to the "expert" (the minister, the Bible, doctrine, rules of order) as the authority to provide us with truth or guidance. In many cases we will be looking to the past (precedent) to seek certainty in making decisions. This has been the traditional view of authority in our society. In many cases, the aim has been to extract absolute answers applicable to all times and people. For that reason it has come to have a negative connotation for many people. This view of authority still dominates so much of our society, but do we need to remain captives of it?

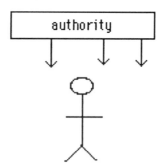

On the other hand, if we ask, "What do I think?", "How do I feel?", or "What do I believe?", then we are declaring that the authority in this instance is internal, in our ability to reason, believe and/or act. Other persons or writings may be regarded as resources, but the final source of decision is the individual and how he or she acquires and uses knowledge. Here, there is a different, but no less firmly established, "absolute" in the absolute commitment to individual choice and decision. The extreme example of this is the declaration that nothing is true unless I decide for myself that it is true.

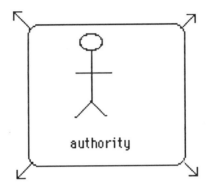

The contrast we have just drawn is too extreme to be realistic. We seldom act in so rigid and divided a fashion. Authority does not simply appear from nowhere and take over our lives. We are not islands. All authority is relational. It is important to note, however, that authority can be exercised in either a dominating or empowering way. Authority, as we have described it thus far, in both its external and internal expression, is authority that is dominating, expressed as "power over." Authority may now be understood as empowering, as "power with" others. It is this view that is the basis of the understanding of authority in this report.

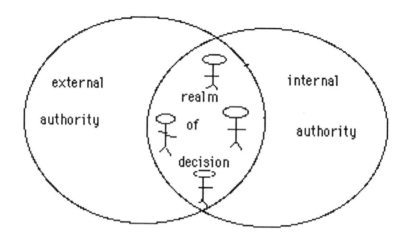

In this view decisions are based on an interaction of internal and external forces of authority, which creates a whole new realm of decision making. Power over another is rejected and any authority that claims to be (or is held up as) absolute is questioned. Likewise, the absolute authority of individual human experience is suspect. Authority is both internal and external and results from a dialogue between what is given and what is felt/believed/known by those in community. We are not free simply to discard or submit to the external or internal authorities. The dialogue between the two, carried on by those in the community, affirms present, past, and future as having value in our decision making and lodges authority in the interaction of internal and external factors expressed in human relationship.

To illustrate, consider the relationship of yourself as a Canadian citizen to a traffic officer who enforces the speed limit. This relationship is not as superficial as we might assume. The authority of the traffic officer is the result of a whole web of interconnected choices about the sort of country you want to live in, the sorts of governments you vote for, the way you learned about authority as a child, and so on. In the "power with" view of authority, you recognize that the authority of the traffic officer is not simply imposed upon you from outside, nor is it an authority you can arbitrarily and unilaterally reject. Instead, you recognize that, along with other citizens, you have decided to be a part of a certain sort of society, and we have named others to maintain the standards that we have chosen to establish. In the same way, you cannot ignore your responsibility to make society as life-affirming and as just as possible. If you become aware of unjust laws, you cannot ignore your responsibility to act for change. Similarly, while we as members of a congregation may recognize the gifts and training of an individual and designate him or her to lead us in understanding the Bible's relationship to our lives (hence giving him or her authority), we have a responsibility to work as a whole community to discover God's Living Word in the scriptural text. The authority of both traffic officer and minister arise out of the life of the community and must be sustained by the community according to standards that the community accepts.

There is a constant tension between the various forces and sources of authority. We need to be alert to the temptation to make any source of authority absolute — a group, an individual, or some other source. As we seek to become more alive to the fulfilling possibilities of Christian community, we come to recognize that the formation of a community of God's faithful is both a gift and a task. Communities include both traditional authority figures and the marginalized; it is in community that relationships of authority are best worked out. In what we do together, we define the shape and nature of authority for ourselves. A graphic, contemporary example of such decision making can be seen in the reaction of Soviet military forces to orders to crush the demonstrations in Moscow in August 1991. It was evident then that the emerging community of soldiers and civilians created a new and more effective form of authority than that exercised by the commanding officers.

On several occasions, The United Church of Canada has affirmed that God has been revealed in a variety of ways. These have included "nature," "history," and the human "heart" (*Basis of Union*, Article II, Of Revelation). It has also affirmed that "Christians of each new generation are called to state [the Church's faith] afresh in terms of the thought of their own age and with the emphasis their age needs" (1940 Statement of Faith, Preamble). In keeping with that call, we can identify at least four sources of Christian faith — heritage, understanding, experience, and the Bible. Different points of view will, of course, place different emphasis on each of the characteristics and may even name others. Elevated alone, each one could become a tyranny leading us away from faith. But if they are held together in creative tension, then each building block of faith is stronger. Each operates with some authority in the life of faith. The first three affect our understanding of scripture. What is their authority in our life? How do they shape our engagement with the Living Word?

HERITAGE:

Heritage is particularly potent for those whose basic confidence is in an external authority. They appeal, with confidence and hope, to the history and doctrines of the church throughout the ages and in the story of The United Church of Canada. An important question to ask constantly is, "Whose heritage?" We must be conscious that not all stories are celebrated and that history is often written by the powerful to the exclusion of others.

UNDERSTANDING:

The various scholarly methods of understanding appeal particularly to those who are committed to an internal authority. The resources of science, scholarship, and critical analysis lead to an intellectual approach and give primacy to individual thought. The potential danger here is of an elitism that excludes, either deliberately or by inference, those without access to scholarly data or techniques.

EXPERIENCE:

As with understanding, experience is often understood as an internal source of authority. This is the case when people say, "This is my experience," as a final appeal to truth. Experience discerned in community, however, recognizes that our understanding of reality is socially constructed. The framework we use for understanding God's actions is shaped by culture, language, class, age, geography, sex, religious affiliation, and so on. Since no two people have identical experiences (and no two cultures either), we must constantly ask whose experience(s) is/are being given authority and why.

BIBLE:

For some, this fourth source is seen as external authority, as a power over us; by others, as internal authority, as a power only when interpreted by individuals; by still others, as power with us, when seen through the interaction of internal and external authorities. The "givenness" of the Bible's authority is being questioned by many who engage it, prompting us to seek a new definition of authority that is appropriate for the Bible's continued meaning in our lives. This does not mean rejecting the Bible as a source of faith, but seeking a new way to engage it as God's Living Word. God speaks in scripture as in other ways, and the Bible points to itself and beyond itself through the mystery of Spirit-inspired writing and interpretation.

How we view each source of authority will be determined by and will determine how we view the other three.

ENGAGING THE BIBLE

One of our tasks in this report is to address the question of the Bible's authority. However, to ask the question "What is the authority of the Bible?" is not a helpful place to begin our discussion. At the outset, we have very little material with which to create an answer. It is more useful to ask, "What does it mean to engage the Bible?" or "Why is it important for the Christian community to wrestle with the message of the Bible?" In this case a variety of answers come to mind:

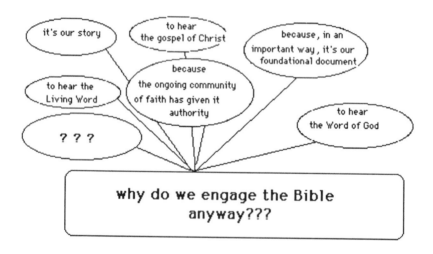

The Bible contains the story that helps shape us into the community we are, a community that extends both in time and geography to include all who have undertaken this journey of faith. The church engages the Bible because it is the foundational story for us as we attempt to understand life, God, and relationships. It is our story, inspired by the Spirit, and hallowed by the continual use of the ongoing community through which we seek to discover God's Living Word.

When we speak of "the Bible's authority," it is helpful to distinguish at least two factors. First, to what does the phrase "the authority of the Bible" actually refer? It could mean: the words of the biblical text; the power of our view of the Bible developed over many years from different sources; the power of our memories of the Bible (not simply the text but the way in which certain portions were used in Sunday school, funerals, family devotions, etc.); the force of another person's interpretation of the Bible. We need to wrestle with the question, "Are we giving authority to the Bible or to our vision or memory of the Bible?" The solution to that question is revealed when Bible study demonstrates that the text of the Bible actually says something very different than what our memories indicate. What we do as a result of those new insights shows us a great deal about where authority lies for us. What are we prepared to allow to have power over us? Is it our memory of what the text means, or the actual text as engaged within community and in dynamic interaction with the other sources of faith?

Second, questions about the interpretation of scripture and the authority of scripture are integrally related. When we read or hear or say the phrase "the Bible says," we must remember that we are dealing with interpretation: what one reader or community understands the Bible to say. Thus, the question of the authority of the Bible becomes interwoven with the question of a particular interpreter's authority. This interweaving of authorities is unavoidable, but it is worth keeping in mind when we discuss questions of power and authority.

STANDARDS OF EVALUATION FOR THE CHRISTIAN COMMUNITY

Many forces and factors operate with authority in our lives. How do we discern the actions of God's Spirit in the midst of these sometimes conflicting claims? How do we discern authority in experience, heritage, understanding, and the text of the Bible itself? How does scripture have authority in the Christian community? Throughout history, various standards have been used to weigh competing claims. Whatever standards we adopt, whether within the Bible's pages or not, we must recognize that all such standards are time bound. One standard is the degree to which an authority conforms to the vision of justice for the whole creation found in Isaiah, which "neither hurts nor destroys in all my holy mountain" but adds to "the knowledge of God in the whole created earth" (Isaiah 9:11). A similar standard is to declare that whatever produces "love, peace, joy, patience, kindness, goodness, faithfulness, gentleness and self-control" is of the Spirit (Galatians 5:22-31). Sometimes, deciding on where we should grant authority is a difficult and ambiguous task. In the often painful ambiguity of discernment, we declare our faith that we are not alone for God is with us, and that it has often been in the wilderness of uncertainty and struggle that God's people have most clearly heard and been empowered by the call of God.

In keeping with our scriptural interpretations, the best features of our heritage, the insights of our understanding, and the encounters with God in our experience, we suggest the following standards of evaluation for any claim to authority:

GOD'S HISTORIC SELF-REVELATION IN JESUS CHRIST IS CRUCIAL IN ESTABLISHING WHAT HAS LEGITIMATE AUTHORITY IN CHRISTIAN COMMUNITY.

LEGITIMATE AUTHORITY, IN EVERY CASE, ENHANCES COMMUNITY OF THE WHOLE CREATED EARTH.

THE WORD OF GOD, IN EVERY CASE, IS LARGER THAN THE TEXT OF THE BIBLE.

For Christians, God's gracious self-revelation in the historic reality of Jesus Christ is the lens through which we must see and the scale by which we must weigh anything that claims authority in relation to us. That includes potentially conflicting passages of scripture. Furthermore, we cannot imagine ourselves to be separate from all creation or community. Such an understanding is unfaithful to the biblical witness. An authority, therefore, which claims to be of God and yet advances one group at the clear expense of another or advances only certain people within a group is wrong. Finally, we do not hold that the word of God is identical to scripture's text. If this were so, then we would still be following exactly the dietary laws or the farming regulations of Leviticus and the prescriptions for church organization and order in the letters of Paul. Instead, we recognize that the word of God, instead of being the textual law that binds us, is the story of faith that has formed us. Our challenge and our call, therefore, is to recognize in the biblical text the signposts which point us to the Living Word of God. This Word, while related to the text, draws us beyond it to the faithful pilgrimage of daily living.

How can God speak to us authoritatively through the written text of scripture today? No matter how we understand and employ them, methods of understanding, experience, and heritage all play a role in our engagement with the Bible. In affirming the interactive sense of authority—scripture as power with us—we are affirming that there will be a degree of ambiguity in our knowledge of scripture and diversity in our interpretation of it. We are also declaring that not all parts of scripture are equally authoritative for us. We confess that we are part of a heritage that has, all too often, abused the Bible by using it to create or perpetuate actions and structures of oppression and domination.

In discerning the authoritative message of scripture we have identified the following tools: methods of understanding, heritage, and experience.

UNDERSTANDING:

In engaging the Bible, the community has access to the work of biblical scholars and reflections of members of the community as methods of understanding. They help the community to discern the meaning of a particular text. Within The United Church of Canada, those methods[2] viewed as more consistent with the Methodist and Reformed traditions have found wider acceptance than others. These methods influence our understanding of a biblical text, and through that understanding, affect our life as a faithful community in the world.

HERITAGE:

The story of the church's response to scripture and to any particular passage from the early church onward is our heritage. Our heritage involves the story of that response in the church's liturgical, doctrinal, educational, and daily life (corporate and individual). It also involves our own understanding of, and response to, those traditions and stories.

EXPERIENCE:

The way in which scripture brings insight, empowerment, and conviction to the individual and community is our experience of the

2. See description of various methods in appendix 1.

Living Word. Part of the authority of scripture is found in its "givenness": the fact that the story has been passed down from generation to generation. That passing down has established the trustworthiness of the biblical record, but each person and each generation must struggle to affirm that trustworthiness. Thus, another part of the authority of scripture is found in its relevance to our experience. This relevance may initially be seen as a judging and convicting relevance. The message that truly comes from God is always, and ultimately, transforming and liberating.

SUMMARY

In conclusion then, the authority of the Bible is found:
— in the interrelationship of the individual and the community;
— in the interrelationship of past and present with a shared vision of the future;
— in the struggle to understand God's word for us today;
— in the act of engaging, which confirms or denies that authority;
— in the conviction, liberation, and transformation that it brings to our personal and community lives.

To engage the Bible faithfully is:
— to participate in a discussion of power, justice, and right relationships;
— to engage in a dialogue that is life-affirming;
— to enter into a journey that takes seriously the pain of the world and God's and our response to that pain.

Engaging the Bible is:

— a dynamic activity where we do not simply engage the text but are engaged by it;

— most faithfully done in community;

— enlightened by the power of the Spirit;

— authoritative when it is experienced as liberating.

III

CONVICTIONS

Having consulted members of the United Church and representatives of other denominations, the Theology and Faith Committee offers the following six convictions. These convictions grow out of our ongoing conversations since 1988 and seek to faithfully reflect that entire important process.

Each conviction is interdependent with all the other convictions. The nearness of each conviction to the others is an indication of that interrelatedness. The convictions are not numbered, because no one conviction is more important than any other. As a result of this interrelatedness, each conviction takes on greater significance when it is examined in harmony with the others. No conviction should be considered in isolation, for the total meaning of the group is greater than the sum of the individual convictions.

The convictions are written in the form of affirmations. Individual and corporate affirmations of our faith, in all aspects of our personal and community life, are important features of the Christian pilgrimage.

Each conviction begins with the introductory phrase, "God calls us to engage the Bible." This phrase is an important way of highlighting who it is that calls us to the enterprise of faith and what it is we do when we engage the Bible. It is God who calls us, through the infinity of grace, to the task of bearing witness to God's redeeming and active love in all creation. We have used the word "engage" to describe our interaction with the Bible because of its multiple layers of meaning.[3] We felt the need for a word that encompassed the differing ways in which scripture is encountered by those who are formed into community by it. Certainly we read the Bible, but we do more than simply read it: we interact with it on several levels. In those interactions, there is two-way communication in which scripture acts upon us to convict, inspire, and empower, and we act upon it, seeking to discern its meaning for our lives and for the life of the communities of which we are a part.

GOD CALLS US TO ENGAGE THE BIBLE AS FOUNDATIONAL AUTHORITY AS WE SEEK TO LIVE THE CHRISTIAN LIFE.

For Christians, the Bible continues to be the predominant witness to belief in God's liberating and transforming activity. With scripture,[4] generations of people from diverse cultural, ethnic, and racial backgrounds have opened their understanding of God's historical and current activity. In scripture, they have been led to see

---

3. We recognize that no word perfectly captures our relationship with the Bible. After much discussion the committee has chosen the word "engage," even though we are aware of some of the negative connotations, such as "hire to do one's bidding" or "bring into conflict."

4. We are aware that other faith communities have their own scripture. In this document, we use the word "scripture" to refer to the Bible.

in their own lives confirmations of God's continued action. In scripture, they have discovered that God's historic self-revelation in Jesus Christ is crucial in establishing what has legitimate authority in the Christian community. Thus, scripture shapes us as a community of God's people. We turn to it in our struggle to understand God's convicting, liberating, and transforming Word for us today and to pass on the story to subsequent generations. In this activity, we can observe the ongoing working of God's Spirit with the people of God.

GOD CALLS US TO ENGAGE THE BIBLE AS A CHURCH SEEKING GOD'S COMMUNITY WITH ALL PEOPLE, LIVING CREATURES, AND THE EARTH.

Having acknowledged that scripture is the foundational story of our community, with power to convict, liberate, and transform, and having acknowledged that legitimate authority in every case enhances community and the whole created earth, we believe that scripture cannot be faithfully engaged in isolation from the larger community of God's people. By this we mean that, even when individuals study the scriptures for devotional, academic, or other reasons, they remain part of the communities that shape them. Throughout history the communities that have shaped God's people have been quite diverse, yet the sharing of the same story has united them into the larger community of God's people. In living with the story, the Christian community has claimed it as scripture. When we engage scripture, we too become part of that historical community. Each of us must also test our personal understanding of scripture against that of the whole community today.

The term "community" may be problematic for those who do not experience community as nurturing or life-giving. At times, the dominant community has subjugated other communities. We need to acknowledge that scripture itself has been used in this process of oppression. The church is not exempt from such a charge. As a community largely characterized by privilege, The United Church of Canada must recognize its past wrongs and recommit itself to the struggle for justice for all in church and in society. We are challenged to seek and to follow the way of Jesus, who gave central place to the marginalized and the poor in his ministry. In turn, we seek to share in the struggles of others and, together, seek God's gracious community for all. We must also seek to liberate scripture from all oppressive use.

God calls us to live in communities of love and justice. More and more, we must recognize that we are shaped by our communities and that, if our faithfulness is to be complete, a major component of our God-given communities must be God's creation, including all living creatures and the earth. This part of our total context must be taken in all seriousness whenever we engage scripture.

GOD CALLS US TO ENGAGE THE BIBLE TO EXPERIENCE THE LIBERATING AND TRANSFORMING WORD OF GOD.

We believe that in every engagement with scripture we expect to hear the message of God's liberating and transforming activity. Liberation is the power of God to free us from those forces that oppress and estrange us from God, God's community, and God's creation. Transformation is the activity of divine grace within us that changes individuals and communities. For Christians, these activities are uniquely personified in Jesus of Nazareth. However, God's liberating and transforming activity is also seen in the lives and writings of the Jewish people prior to Jesus and in the witness of the people of God since the time of Jesus.

We all need to experience liberation and transformation. In the dominant Western Christian tradition, this has generally been understood to be liberation from individual sin and death and a transformation to a new way of life. Today we need to affirm different streams within this dominant tradition, as well as other traditions that have understood sin as a social condition. Oppressive systems and structures that have caused and perpetuated sin must be transformed. Often, Christians have been part of those systems and structures experienced by others as oppressive. The call to liberation and transformation comes to both the powerless and the powerful and, always, the liberation of the former is linked to the transformation of the latter.

Periodically, the Christian church has ignored the need to liberate the Bible itself from oppressive uses. For example, for too long we did not oppose the use of scripture to deny ordination to women or to oppress people of colour. As members of the United Church continue the struggle to live out the Christian faith today, we need to recognize and confess those times when we have participated in structures of oppression and when we need to be transformed by the liberating word of God.

GOD CALLS US TO ENGAGE THE BIBLE WITH AN AWARENESS OF OUR THEOLOGICAL, SOCIAL, AND CULTURAL ASSUMPTIONS.

Our understanding of scripture is filtered through our assumptions. Having assumptions is neither right nor wrong, it is simply a function of being human. These assumptions may broadly be termed theological, social, or cultural. We are often unaware of these assumptions. Therefore, it is essential to endeavor to name them and clarify their influence in our lives. For example, a theological assumption (one related to how we understand God and what it means to be human in creation) may centre around belief in a literal, physical virgin birth for Jesus. One person may assume that accepting such a belief is crucial for Christian faithfulness, while another may attach no importance to such a belief. A social assumption (one related to our place in society) may centre the health and wholeness of a person on a certain level of material and social success, or it may regard such a level of success as a state arising from exploitation and oppression of others. A cultural assumption (one related to identities, values or meanings) may attach greater or lesser importance to the place of one's cultural or ethnic origins.

Although other assumptions are beginning to be heard, the dominant assumption about Christianity is that it is Western, white, hierarchical, and biased toward the masculine. Other voices can help us identify our assumptions, and we must commit ourselves to listening to them. Listening to others and examining our assumptions in the light of theirs brings us to a new understanding and appreciation of both. When we truly enter into conversation with others, we know that we risk being changed by the power of God's Spirit. In such an interchange we seek not to break the spirit of others but to honour and respect them, even while inviting them to join us in responding to God's invitation to liberation and transformation.

Our assumptions do not release us from the Christian challenge of engaging with scripture nor from the search, with others, for God's community of justice and love. Indeed, having our assumptions identified, challenged, and perhaps changed enriches us. God's invitation to us is to cherish the differences we encounter and to avoid the risks of isolation and imprisonment that come from refusing to expose our own assumptions. The challenge of living with ambiguities and the possibility of being confronted and changed can be painful. Many find the pain too great to bear. Yet God invites us to embrace that special pain and be enriched by it, as in encounters with others we seek to become part of God's larger community.

GOD CALLS US TO ENGAGE THE BIBLE WITH A SENSE OF SACRED MYSTERY AND IN DYNAMIC INTERACTION WITH HUMAN EXPERIENCE, UNDERSTANDING, AND HERITAGE.

In the encounter with scripture, as in the encounter with God, we also "see through a glass darkly," because the word of God, in every case, is larger than the text of the Bible. Scripture itself refers to many of its teachings as divine secrets, the meanings of which are not entirely revealed to us. There is a holiness in the experience of encountering God in scripture that we must treasure. When engaging scripture, we walk on holy ground. Thus, as we engage the scriptures, awe and wonder should set the tone of our involvement. It is a mystery, as well, that, through human experience, understanding, and heritage, we can gain further insight into God's Word. Furthermore, when these three interact with one another and with scripture, we receive yet another gift of insight, for the relationship among the three is dynamic, each affecting the others, bringing new and transformed meaning. We must always be aware of whose experience, whose understanding, and whose heritage we are employing. As we engage the Bible in this way, we believe that God's revelation of the sacred mystery will continue. We also experience the sacred mystery in the connections between our personal and collective lives, the recorded and oral history of the church, recorded scripture and our understanding. This confirms our understanding that truth is relational and our conviction that God's Spirit is active in all four sources of faith: heritage, understanding, experience, and the Bible.

To emphasize sacred mystery is to deny neither the important contributions of scholars nor the interpretive gifts of those without formal education or privilege. We recognize that God works, as in the past, through the lives of common, ordinary people, as well as through appointed teachers and scholars. The various critical methods of scholarship (see appendix 1) add new dimensions to our understanding of God's liberating and transforming activity. They help us to understand the context of the scripture and to see its relevance to our life situation in new ways. Always, however, we must seek to be attentive to that which is outside our human sources, to the sacred mystery which lies beyond experience, understanding, and heritage.

GOD CALLS US TO ENGAGE THE BIBLE TRUSTING GOD'S SPIRIT TO ENLIVEN OUR UNDERSTANDING AND TO EMPOWER OUR ACTING.

The Spirit who breathed life-giving air into the nostrils of humanity has also breathed life-giving power into both the writing and the engaging of scripture. As we engage scripture, that same Spirit can bring us life-giving understanding. God has acted in history and continues to be revealed in scripture, in creation, and through the lives of God's people, including their written works, since the closing of the scriptural canon. Although this continued involvement and revelation is part of the ongoing mystery of faith, we trust in the Spirit's presence as we work together to discern the meaning of scripture for our faith and action in the world.

In the sometimes painful ambiguity of discernment, we declare our faith that we are not alone; God is with us. It has often been in the wilderness of uncertainty and struggle that God's people have most clearly engaged and been empowered by the call of God.

If we are to hear God's call and experience God's liberation and transformation, then we must engage the scripture on a regular basis. This is a crucial part of our faithful participation in the community of God's people. Regularly engaging scripture, with the fullest possible awareness of our assumptions, allows us to connect again and again with the authority that breathes meaning into our Christian life and our interactions with God, people, and all creation. As we engage the scripture, using all of our God-inspired resources of heritage, understanding, and experience in the holy and awesome mystery of faith, we are inspired, transformed, and empowered to live as God's community with all creation.

IV

INSIGHTS AND IMPLICATIONS

Theory and practice cannot be separated in our efforts to do theology. Theological statements gain greater acceptance within the church when serious attention is given to their application. Assessment of truth, in other words, rests not only on the question "Does it make sense"? but also on the questions "What then? What effect does it have on or with the community of faith in its witness in the world?"

This chapter looks briefly at the latter question. It is an attempt to draw out some of the implications of our stated convictions about engaging the Bible. In doing so, the intention is not to be exhaustive but illustrative, with the hope that similar attempts will be made by congregations, groups, and individuals, as they seek to apply the convictions in their particular location.

The committee's approach was to deal with the convictions collectively rather than separately. Thus, there is no particular order to the insights and narrative of implications that follow. The quotations are illustrative materials intended to provoke further reflection on the insights.

INSIGHT: **Engaging the Bible is not optional for the Christian Community.**

The convictions associate the Bible very closely with being the Church. To be the Church is to take the Bible seriously as the Church's central book and trustworthy source for hearing God's Living Word. It is not to be treated as just one more addition on the shelf of our reference library or of ornamental significance in the home. It is essential in our seeking to be a community of and for God in our time. It is to be treated not only as an inspired book but a book that continues, through God's Spirit, to inspire us in discerning God's will for our lives. Furthermore, the convictions imply that the Bible belongs to everyone, to the Church as a whole, and that it must not remain, in perception or in fact, the book of the professional minister.

> *Why is it that the vast majority of Christian believers remain largely unexposed to Christian learning — to historical-critical studies of the Bible, to the content and structure of the great doctrines, to two thousand years of classic works on the Christian life, to basic disciplines of theology, biblical languages, Christian ethics? Why do bankers, lawyers, farmers, physicians, homemakers, scientists, salespeople, managers of all sorts, people who carry out all kinds of complicated tasks in their work and home, remain at a literalist, elementary school level in their religious understanding? How is it that high school age church members move easily and quickly into the complex world of computers, foreign languages, DNA,*

and calculus, and cannot even make a beginning in historical-critical interpretations of a single text of Scripture? How is it possible one can attend or even teach in a Sunday school for decades and at the end of that time lack the interpretive skills of someone who has taken three or four weeks in an introductory course in Bible at a university or seminary? (Edward Farley, "Can Church Education be Theological Education?" in *Theology Today*, vol. XLII, no. 2 [1985], 164.)

What Could This Mean for You?

How might your congregation seek a more intentional biblical perspective for its life and work?

Examples: Appoint, for each meeting of a committee, board, or Session, someone to take leadership in bringing theological and biblical reflection to the meeting.

Your church board is being asked to make a decision on the future use of the building (day care facility, political campaign offices, etc.). Or, there is growing concern by some members about the use of the building for weddings unrelated to the congregation's life and work. Explore the use of the Bible in taking action on these matters.

Work with the ministerial staff and other resource persons to seek out helpful exegetical resources in preparation for the task.

Explore with the Session (Worship and Liturgy committee, or other) the use of the Bible in your worship life, through biblical preaching, use of drama, story telling, etc....

Other?

How might your congregation become empowered in the use of the Bible?

Examples: Set up a special task group (or work with the Christian Education Committee) to explore ways, in consultation with the ministerial staff, to educate the membership of the church about the history of the Bible and methods of interpretation, so that all may have more confidence in the use of the scriptures.

Meet with the ministerial staff to discuss ways the professionalization of the Bible, in terms of clergy training only, may be countered, so that the Bible may become open to all members.

Talk with those involved in community activity and discuss with them ways that the Bible may be or is a resource for them.

Through the Session, set up a roster of lay readers, inclusive of all ages, with a balance of women and men.

Explore with the educational and resource centres, presbytery, conference, and General Council Divisions ways in which all members may know the biblical story and how that story can have an influence on their own stories.

Challenge the Session or appropriate committee to discover ways for all members to take their learning seriously.

Other?

Why did I have to wait until I was forty to discover and learn about the importance of sources/authors/community context? The one issue which is not addressed in this document ... is the issue of why the principles of biblical interpretation and of hermeneutics have not been shared more honestly and courageously by the ministry who have been privy to this information for decades, if not generations. Why the collusion between ministry and congregations to not bring these difficult and challenging issues out into the open? (From a congregational response to the Study Document.)

INSIGHT: **When we engage the Bible, individually and collectively, we are deeply influenced by and entangled in the world-views of the particular nation/community/family in which we live.**

The convictions stress the fact that engagement of the Bible is always within a particular location. We come from particular backgrounds of thought and practice that make our knowledge not only incomplete but biased. Awareness of this location, and of the horizon of understanding that is within it, is essential for any individual or community seeking a biblical perspective. Our particular situation in life offers both gift and challenge when we seek God's Word through scripture.

> *Northern arrogance is one of our main difficulties at the present time. We are so self-confident that we assume that our own societies, if not perfect, are close to it, that our way of doing things, our own industrial advancement should be the model for others. This is arrogant because it's wrong, totally insensitive to the great strengths of other cultures, and because it does not recognize or reflect the peculiar geographic and historical circumstances of individual countries.* (Ivan Head, Professor of International Relations at University of British Columbia as quoted in the *Toronto Star*, July 20, 1991.)

What Could This Mean for You?

How might you undergo a process of self-discovery as a congregation so that you are aware of who you are in relation to others in the community, country, and world?

Examples: Request the Session (through its appropriate committee) to seek out resources that may help the congregation do contextual analysis.

Set up a series of educational / informational evenings to help members of the congregation discover the diversities of tradition, economic status, and power within the congregation and the local community. Invite a person who would be able to help you look at the interpretation of scripture from a feminist perspective.

Seek out resources that deal with the subject of sexism and racism and how they have influenced the church's thinking and engagement with the Bible. Work towards a congregational position on sexual harassment and/or the 500 years celebration of the discovery of America by Columbus.

Other?

Long before my people journeyed to this land, your people were here, and you received from your elders an understanding of creation, and of the mystery that surrounds us all that was deep and rich and to be treasured. We did not hear you when you shared your vision. In our zeal to tell you of the good news of Jesus Christ we were closed to the value of your spirituality. We confused western ways and culture with the depth and breadth and length and height of the gospel of Christ. We imposed our civilization as a condition of accepting gospel. We tried to make you be like us and in so doing we helped to destroy the vision that made you what you were. As a result, you, and we, are poorer and the image of the Creator in us is twisted, blurred and we are not what we are meant by God to be. We ask you to forgive us and to walk together with us in the spirit of Christ so that our peoples may be blessed and God's creation healed. (The United Church of Canada, "Apology to Native Peoples," from *Spirit of Gentleness* [Toronto: UCC, 1989], 9.)

INSIGHT: **Our interpretation of scripture is most clearly shown in the way we live.**

The convictions challenge us to look seriously at the consequences of our engagement with the Bible. They point to the fact that the claim to hear God's Word within the scriptures is linked with what happens to people's lives, the earth, and its creatures as a result of this engagement. We are encouraged by the convictions to ask some of the following questions: What effect is our reading as a community going to have on those who are socially and/or economically deprived? How freeing and/or humanizing is our engagement going to be for women? For children? For people of colour? The convictions are urging us to affirm that engagement with the Bible is always on the side of life and its fulfillment for all.

Paul Gifford speaks about the 'health gospel' that is being spread about Africa today by fundamentalist Christian groups. The proponents base the doctrine on a particular reading of certain biblical texts. The texts most frequently cited are Deut. 28-30, Mk 11:23-24, Acts 3:6, Acts 5:12-16 and others. All a Christian has to do is believe, and claim his or her health by expressing that belief. "This

Christianity leaves everything up to God and it focuses only on the health of an individual, ignoring the needs of the nation. This Christianity leads to no analysis of the social-political causes of deteriorating health services (e.g., economic mismanagement, destabilization, corruption, diverting available resources, military spending or to prestige projects) . . . This Christianity leaves oppressive structures completely unchallenged." (Paul Gifford, *Christianity: To Save or Enslave?* [Harare Zimbabwe: Ecumenical Documentation and Information Centre of Eastern and Southern Africa, 1990], 12.)

What Could This Mean for You?

How might the congregation learn about, and be supported in, engaging the Bible as an instrument of liberation for people?

Examples: Become familiar with how and where the Bible has been used to oppress and enslave people. Learn from some of the Native peoples in Canada how they experienced the Bible in the hands of early Canadian missionaries.

Encourage members to share with one another their experiences of feeling oppressed by the use of the Bible.

Review some of the benchmarks established by the 30th General Council for our social justice work.

How do they relate to the biblical vision of relationship with our neighbour?

Seek out ways to have conversation with the poor and explore the meaning of passages such as Isaiah 61 and Luke 1:46-55.

Explore with women the meaning of such texts as 2 Samuel 13:1-22 or Judges 19.

... that the needs of the poor have priority over the wants of the rich, the freedom of the dominated must have priority over the liberty of the powerful and that the participation of the marginalized must take priority over the preservation of an order that excludes them. (Division of Mission in Canada, "Resolution No. 42," from *Record of Proceedings of the Thirtieth General Council* [Toronto: UCC, 1988], 326.)

INSIGHT: **Interpretation is unavoidable when we are engaging the Bible.**

The meaning of a biblical text comes in response to the question: What does it mean to me or us? No one text has one meaning for all. The same text may have different meanings for people, depending on who is doing the engaging and the interpretative approach or principle that is being used. Feminists, for example, approach scripture with the full humanity of women as a key principle. Whatever denies or distorts the humanity of women is not received as an authentic word from God. We need to be aware of and acquainted with different interpretative principles as we engage the Bible. An important question is: How does the meaning of the Bible arise for me and my community?

> *Children's Bibles are peculiarly susceptible to nefarious interpretations because they paraphrase scripture.* (William H. Willimon, "What Bible are Your Children Reading?", in *Christian Century* [July 24-31/91] , 709 - 710.)

What Could This Mean for You?

How might your congregation empower the members in the essential task of biblical interpretation?

Examples: Encourage the Session or appropriate committee to purchase appropriate resources that will help develop the skills for interpretation.

Request the Session to develop or acquire an analysis of various translations for the guidance of members, particularly in relation to children's Bible materials. Refer again to the Study Document, *The Authority and Interpretation of Scripture*, pp. 12 - 13.

Request the ministerial staff to design educational courses that will help members understand the challenge and importance of various approaches to scripture.

The *Gospel in Solentiname* is a record and reflection of biblical interpretation by poor farmers and fisherfolk in Solentiname, Nicaragua. In a similar way, create biblical study opportunities for listening to those in your community without formal education or with different educational backgrounds.

Other?

The base of all the reading of the Bible is the people's reading of the Bible. The Bible today for us is authoritative in the people's struggles. Latin America is being integrated as a whole to this reading of the Bible ... different kinds of groups reading in very specific ways ... the black women, the poor women, the children, the youth, the indigenous people, the farm workers. (Comments by a Brazilian during the consultation by members of the Theology and Faith Committee in Brazil, March 1990.)

INSIGHT: **Each interpretation is an invitation to ever new discoveries and insights into God's covenant with life and the earth.**

The convictions remind us that there is something beyond our particular interpretation and pursuit of knowledge, a mystery that lures us to ever new paths of interpretation. They remind us that God's Word cannot be contained in our interpretations of scripture. The reference to sacred mystery in the convictions reminds us that we must seek a biblical perspective prayerfully and with humility, knowing that a completely faithful interpretation is not possible.

> To think about otherness requires that we who make theory slow down our thoughts, stretch out the race to analysis, loosen our grip on the answer, and assume an attitude of humility. (Ruth Smith, "The Evasion of Otherness: A Problem of Feminist Moral Reconstruction," quoted by Marilyn Legge in "Colourful Difference: 'Otherness' and Image of God for Canadian Feminist Theologies" [unpublished].)

What Could This Mean for You?

How might your congregation remain open to the movement of God's Spirit while engaging the Bible?

Examples: Explore with the Session a Bible study that invites openness of opinion and viewpoints, is carried on in the spirit of dialogue, and enters into the "otherness" of different interpretations and sacred religious texts.

Watch for and challenge any interpretation of scripture that stifles discussion or binds one to past biblical engagement and tradition.

Invite dialogue with Native people from your congregation or the wider community in order to experience the gift of their spirituality and its value for biblical engagement.

Create biblical study opportunities in which the gifts of children's voices and insights may be received.

Other?

The image of living on the earth in harmony with creation and therefore with the creator is a helpful one for me. It means "faithful" living in the earth will mean moving in the rhythm of the creation. It will mean vibrating to the pulse of life in a natural way without having to "own" the source of the music. It allows the creator to reveal truth to the creation and all may share in it. (Stan McKay, "Unity of All Life," in *Spirit of Gentleness: Lenten Readings and Prayers*, ed. Joyce Carlson [Toronto: UCC, 1989], 15.)

Many other insights are possible from the convictions. We invite the congregations of The United Church of Canada to continue the journey of discovery. We also invite the church as a whole to ask: "What could these convictions mean to the mission of the church in its national and international life?"

APPENDIX I:

CRITICAL METHODS AND THE BIBLE

A "critical" approach or reading of the Bible means that we ask questions about a text — its history and its meaning in its historical context. We also ask questions about our own context and about our assumptions as Christians living in the twentieth century. Asking questions about the Bible is a faithful work that helps us hear the text more clearly in its original setting. It also allows us to examine and live our own lives more faithfully as God's people in the light of the Bible's story and history.

Historical-criticism is a collection of literary and historical methods that asks questions about the history and meaning of a biblical text. These methods can be applied to any literary work, not just to the Bible. These methods help us to understand how the stories in the Bible came to be in their present form and to see more clearly the significance these stories had for those who first encountered them. We must never assume that these methods answer all the questions we have about the Bible, or about any particular passage; they are specific methods that try to answer specific questions.

We will use the story of Jesus walking on the water, as found in Mark 6:45-53, as an example to illustrate the different critical methods and the specific questions they raise.

HISTORICAL-CRITICAL METHODS

Textual Criticism

The Bible was originally written in the ancient languages of Hebrew and Greek. The aim of textual criticism is to recover the text that is as close as possible to the author's original story. We do not have the original copies of any biblical book. We have only "copies of copies." Turning to our story of Jesus walking on water, some Greek manuscripts have the word "already" after "was" in verse 47. Most textual critics leave it out because it is contained in only a few manuscripts. On the other hand, in verse 50, some manuscripts leave out the words "for they saw him" and move "all" to the end of verse 49 ("and all cried out"). However, most textual critics leave these words in the text (as they are in the Revised Standard Version), because most Greek manuscripts have this wording.

Source Criticism

This method asks whether Mark used any written sources for this story. The source critic points out that this story is also told in Matthew and John (Matthew 14:22-33 and John 6:15-21). Did Mark copy his version from them, or did they copy from him? The majority of source critics agree that Matthew had a copy of Mark when he wrote his Gospel, and that Mark's account was a written source for Matthew, but not for John. This becomes apparent when we notice how much similarity there is between Matthew and Mark, but not between Mark and John. Today this theory is being questioned by some critics who believe that Mark used Matthew's Gospel as a source. Whenever critics try to decide who used whose account, they are doing source criticism.

Redaction Criticism

This method asks how Mark edited his sources and questions the theological concerns or bias in his version of the Gospel story. The redaction critic points out that Mark connects this story (Jesus walking on water) to the story of the Feeding of the Five Thousand (Mark 6: 35-44), since he refers to it in verse 52. The redaction critic notes that Mark's version of the story portrays the disciples as having "hardened hearts" (verse 52). The other Gospel writers are not so hard on the disciples. Mark makes the same point in 8:17 and 21.

Other discoveries in redaction criticism can be seen by comparing Matthew's and John's versions of this story to Mark's. Matthew adds verses about Peter in this story. This happens elsewhere in Matthew but not in Mark or John. Matthew also names Peter in stories when other Gospel writers do not (see Matthew 16:7-20; 17: 24-27).

Form Criticism

This method asks how the stories about Jesus and the sayings of Jesus were transmitted in their oral form before they were written down. It also asks what the different settings of the church's life were in which the stories were told. The form critic points out that the story in Mark 6 has similarities to other nature miracle stories about Jesus, such as the Stilling of the Storm (Mark 4: 35-41), and the

Feeding of the Five Thousand, and Four Thousand (Mark 6: 35-44; 8: 1-10). There is an even closer resemblance between this story and the resurrection stories in which Jesus appears to the disciples unexpectedly (see Luke 24:37). Thus, it has some characteristics of an epiphany or appearance of Jesus to the disciples. The form critic notes that amazing stories such as this one, in which Jesus defies or suspends the laws of nature, are also told of important persons in other cultures of that time.

Historical Criticism

This method tries to ascertain the historical event behind the biblical record. This is not always easy to determine. Many stories are told about Jesus that indicate that he was noteworthy or unusual in some sense. The historical critic poses questions about the historical evidence that may or may not confirm events in Jesus' life and ministry. In our example, we note that it was unusual for the disciples to travel out on the sea without Jesus, but it is not impossible to imagine it happening. All three versions (Mark, Matthew, and John) report this incident, which means that Mark did not invent it but that it was passed on to him. It is more important to ask about its meaning or message than its reality as an historical fact.

OTHER METHODS OF INTERPRETATION

The historical-critical methods we have discussed were developed over the period of 150 years before the 1960s. Since then, other interpretative approaches and methods have been introduced to our study of the Bible. These methods do not replace the older ones, but do raise questions about their presuppositions and their approach to the Bible. They focus more on the Bible as a piece of literature. These new methods ask questions about how biblical passages work as stories rather that focusing on their historical context.

Literary Criticism

This method shares some elements with historical-criticism. It examines the use of particular words, phrases, and symbols. It also asks questions about the plot of the story, which characters are involved, and how they interact with one another. For example, our story involves Jesus, the crowd, and the disciples. When we describe in more detail how they relate and what they do, we are doing literary criticism.

Reader-Response Criticism

This approach focuses on the role of the interpreter and asks how he or she finds or creates meaning in the story. The older methods claimed that the meaning lay with the text itself. Reader-response criticism points out that a major part of any interpretation depends on the interpreter. We can see this in how we respond to the story of Jesus walking on water. We listen to the story line, but we also fill in the gaps as we go along. We do this by drawing on our personal experience, our cultural assumptions, and our values. We can ask ourselves (and compare our responses to those of others), "What did the disciples need to learn from the Feeding stories that would help them understand Jesus' walking on water?" Our answers may well reveal many of our assumptions about the story, Jesus, and ourselves.

Materialist Criticism

This approach asks about the social, economical, and even physical dimensions that can be seen in a Bible passage. It challenges us to look at our own social and physical situation as interpreters. In the story of Jesus walking on water, we notice that the events take place in a rural area, not in a city. Jesus is a peasant carpenter's son, who is associated with fisherfolk and the lower levels of society. From a materialist point of view, our concern is to identify the social classes to be found among the disciples and those with whom Jesus comes into contact. In this approach, it is important to note that the disciples think they see a ghost, not a real person. The ghost is on the water, not the land. These material aspects of the story remind us that the story deals with real people and real elements of nature. A materialist reading raises serious questions for us if our politics, economics, and theology somehow reduce other people to a ghost-like existence or if we treat the earth's elements as things to be ignored or overcome.

Feminist Criticism

Essentially, this approach seeks to read biblical passages from a woman's perspective and with women's concerns in mind. We note that the story of Jesus walking on water deals exclusively with men, as do most of the Gospel stories. "The Disciples" in Mark are always the twelve (3: 13-19), although we know that there were women to be found among the followers of Jesus (Mark 15: 40-41; 16: 1-8; Luke 8:1-3). The Gospel of Mark contains some stories that include women (Mark 1: 29-31; 5: 24-34), and Luke includes many more. A feminist reading calls us to explore and challenges us to evaluate our own assumptions about women in the community of faith and to search out the accounts of women in the biblical record.

APPENDIX II:

RESPONSES TO THE AUTHORITY AND INTERPRETATION OF SCRIPTURE STUDY DOCUMENT

RURAL:

Individual Responses	33
Sessional Responses	154
Group Responses	194
Total Rural Responses	381

SMALL TOWN:

Individual Responses	42
Sessional Responses	85
Group Responses	133
Total Small Town Responses	260

URBAN:
Individual Responses   37
Sessional Responses   41
Group Responses   168
Total Urban Responses   246

SUBURBAN:
Individual Responses   32
Sessional Responses   31
Group Responses   95
Total Suburban Responses   158

INNER CITY:
Individual Responses   31
Sessional Responses   10
Group Responses   31
Total Inner City Responses   72

NEW CHURCH DEVELOPMENT:
Individual Responses   5
Sessional Responses   3
Group Responses   1
Total New Church Development Responses   9

CONFERENCES:
No response

PRESBYTERIES:
                                                               2

CONTINUING EDUCATION CENTRES:
No response

THEOLOGICAL SCHOOLS:
Individual Responses | 2
Group Responses | 0

ECUMENICAL RESPONSES:
Canadian InterChurch | 5
Canadian InterFaith | 0
Other Country | 4

INDIVIDUAL RESPONSES
(not classified under Pastoral Charge):
Ordained | 13
Lay | 15
Saff | 1

OTHER RESPONSES (not classified anywhere above): | 54

TOTAL INDIVIDUAL RESPONSES | 180

TOTAL SESSIONAL RESPONSES | 324

TOTAL OTHER GROUP RESPONSES | 622

TOTAL NON-PASTORAL CHARGE RESPONSES | 96

TOTAL RESPONSES TO THE DOCUMENT | **1,222**

REPONSES CLASSIFIED IN TERMS OF CONFERENCE AND PRESBYTERY

Conference	**Presbytery**	
Newfoundland	Avalon	6
& Labrador	Humber	7
	Labrador	2
	St. John's	1
	Terra Nova	11
	TOTAL	27
Maritime	Bermuda	
	Chignecto	18
	Halifax	15
	Inverness-Guysborough	5
	Miramachi	5
	Pictou	5
	Prince Edward Island	20
	Saint John	9
	St. Stephen	3
	South Shore	8
	Sydney	3
	Truro	9
	Valley	2
	Woolastook	13
	TOTAL (+ 1)	116

Montreal & Ottawa	Laurentien	
	Montreal	15
	Ottawa	50
	Quebec-Sherbrooke	7
	Seaway Valley	18
	TOTAL (+1)	91
Bay of Quinte	Belleville	18
	Cobourg	5
	Kingston	14
	Lindsay	6
	Oshawa	15
	Peterborough	11
	Renfrew	8
	TOTAL (+1)	77
Toronto	Dufferin & Peel	9
	Grey	13
	Muskoka	12
	Simcoe	17
	Toronto Don Valley	14
	Toronto Scarborough	6
	Toronto South	22
	Toronto West	7
	York	11
	TOTAL	111

Hamilton	Bruce	13
	Erie	9
	Halton	30
	Hamilton	16
	Niagara	7
	Waterloo	30
	TOTAL (+1)	106
London	Algoma	12
	Elgin	3
	Essex	21
	Huron-Perth	28
	Kent	11
	Lambton	10
	Middlesex	38
	Oxford	7
	TOTAL	130
Manitou	Cochrane	10
	North Bay	10
	Sudbury	8
	Temiskaming	5
	TOTAL	33
Manitoba	Birtle	9
& N.W. Ontario	Brandon	12
	Cambrian	8
	Carman	5

	Northland	8
	Portage La Prairie	7
	Selkirk	11
	Winnipeg	30
	TOTAL (+2)	92
Saskatchewan	Battleford	11
	Cypress Hills	5
	Moose Jaw	4
	Prince Albert	10
	Qu'Appelle	6
	Regina	16
	Rosetown	5
	Saskatoon	21
	Souris Valley	11
	Yorkton	10
	TOTAL (+1)	100
Alberta & Northwest	Calgary	28
	Coronation	6
	Edmonton	22
	Foothills	4
	Peace River	3
	Red Deer	14
	St. Paul	6
	South Alberta	37
	Yellowhead	18
	TOTAL	138

British Columbia	Cariboo	4
	Comox-Nanaimo	10
	Fraser	23
	Kamloops-Okanagan	13
	Kootenay	10
	Prince Rupert	3
	Vancouver-Burrard	8
	Vancouver-South	10
	Victoria	15
	Westminster	22
	TOTAL (+2)	120
All Native Circle	All Tribes	0
	Keewatin	0
	Plains	0

APPENDIX III:

HIGHLIGHTS FROM THE AUTHORITY AND INTERPRETATION OF SCRIPTURE PRESENTATION TO THE 34TH GENERAL COUNCIL

Presented by David MacLachlan, Margaret MacPherson, Marilyn Legge, John Young, and Hallett Llewellyn for the Theology and Faith Committee.

This report is the product of consultation, listening, and an attempt to perceive and lift up the role of the Bible in our lives. It seeks to open the Bible, not shut it down. It is the product of listening to voices — it is not an Angus Reed poll! It is where we are and where we need to go. It is the result of participation with the whole committee, the whole United Church of Canada, and our ecumenical partners. This study was not top down or a think-tank, yet it says something different about the present and the direction for the future. The last report was the trees, and this one is the forest! ... tributaries to the river of biblical life in The United Church of

Canada. The Bible is central to the life and work of The United Church of Canada.

The committee addressed the authority of the Bible and its role in our lives, *not* Christology; yet we lift up the centrality of Jesus Christ to God's work and the Bible's story—but not exclusively. We did not say all there is to say; yet the report has important convictions and insights. Nor have we tried to do your Bible study for you; you will have to do your own chewing. We recognize that the Bible's authority is not just in what we read in it. Its authority is also in the context in which we live its message.

We invite you to experience something of the process and experience the committee has seen and heard in preparing the report. Listen now to some of the voices we have heard.[5]

The serious question has never been whether the Bible is primary authority for Christian faith and life but what sort of authority it is. Christian faith is no sedative for world-weary souls, no knapsack of ready answers to life's deepest questions. Instead, Christian faith prompts questions and fights the inclination to accept things as they are.

In the report *The Authority and Interpretation of Scripture*, there are three standards or criteria of evaluation for any claim to authority to help sort out what truly belongs to Christian faith.

Theologian Avery Dulles defines authority as "that which (or those whom) one has reason to trust."[6] Scripture is indispensable in

---

5. At this point in the presentation, a video was shown of the consultation by members of the Theology and Faith Committee with members of various denominations in Brazil in March 1990. Several excerpts from congregational responses to the Study Document were read to Council. The chapter of this document that contained these responses, "Listening to the Voices," has been deleted from this publication by action of General Council for cost reasons. If you would like a copy of "Listening to the Voices," contact the Secretary for Theology and Faith in the General Council office.

6. Avery Dulles, *Scripture in the Jewish and Christian Traditions*, ed. F. Greenspahn (Nashville: Abingdon Press, 1982), 14.

bringing us into a trustworthy relationship with the living God through Jesus Christ by the power of the Holy Spirit, and thus into relationship with others and the entire Creation. To speak of the authority of the Bible is to speak of its life-giving power, which by God's Spirit helps create and nourish this new life in community, in relationship with God and the created order. Now let us look at each standard or criteria.

GOD'S HISTORIC SELF-REVELATION IN JESUS CHRIST IS CRUCIAL IN ESTABLISHING WHAT HAS LEGITIMATE AUTHORITY IN CHRISTIAN COMMUNITY.

The Theology and Faith Committee affirms that the presence of God embodied by Jesus Christ is transmitted through the prism of the biblical witness. It beckons and challenges Christians into relationship with the living God attested to in the Bible.

The Bible *is* our unique, primary source for our knowledge of God. In it we discover the tangible well-being — salvation or wholeness — people experience by being in touch with Jesus Christ, God-with-us. So, for Christians, the life of Jesus of Nazareth and the risen Christ are central. How we tell what is of Christ is based on the poor person who loved and suffered among all; who showed us how to be more capable of loving; who moved towards the Kingdom of God where there are no excluded ones; who lived free from having and for living; who lives on among us as the resurrected Christ whenever we embrace the gift of abundant life and pass it on.

LEGITIMATE AUTHORITY, IN EVERY CASE, ENHANCES COMMUNITY OF THE WHOLE CREATED EARTH.

While scripture witnesses to God and Jesus Christ and the Holy Spirit in relationship with the people of Israel and the early church, it is not identical with God. Christians do not believe in the Bible; we believe in the God who is witnessed to in it. Because the Bible is as human and sacred as we are today, not everything found in the Bible is to be taken as a direct word of God to us.

Some texts of the Bible may stand in utmost tension with the liberation of divine-human relation that Jesus embodied. We cannot deny, for example, that scripture contains militaristic and patriarchal ideas. We need authority precisely for the purpose of helping us discover, recover, empower, and encourage ourselves and one another to live by God, into the promise of new and abundant life present in Jesus Christ.

So, authority today is to be tested by the kind of tangible, spiritual well-being it sustains in ways that point to what Jesus called the Kingdom of God.

THE WORD OF GOD, IN EVERY CASE, IN LARGER THAN THE TEXT OF THE BIBLE.

Authority is neither simply outside us nor inside us; authority is generated by cooperation with God in relationship to our struggles for freedom and justice and peace. For Christians, then, true authority is never coercive but invitational. Therefore, we draw on biblical authority in relation to the rest of our faith heritage, as well as our best judgments or reason and imagination, in living responsibly in our time and place. The Bible cannot stand alone.

Our United Church tradition recognizes this fact when we affirm that the Bible is our sacred text, but not in the sense that the Bible was actually written by God. The second Article of Faith in the 1925 Basis of Union says that the Bible *contains* the word of God. For example, no theologian, dead or alive, none of us here, equates the importance of the exodus or Jesus' death and resurrection with that of the instructions for building the tabernacle of the Ark. Hence, the Basis of Union does not say that the Bible *is* the word of God, but that it contains it.

In short, *we* are left to discern what is the word of God today. The Bible points beyond itself to the reality of God in our church and world. The Bible is our resource for faith and freedom if it inspires us to envision and embody relationships of justice and mutuality, of care and respect, and to resist domination, subordination, violence, and greed. The Bible is not the word of God when it is used to justify structures and dynamics of unjust relationships. Jesus did not die 2,000 years ago and leave us a book. God lives on with us and acts through us still, guided and empowered by Christ's Spirit, to find bread, not stones, as we study the Bible, as we try to understand how it contributes to our redemption, to our liberation from sin and suffering, and to the healing of the world.

As a committee we believe the six convictions are interdependent. We also believe that the convictions are directly related to the three criteria for evaluating claims of authority.

GOD CALLS US TO ENGAGE THE BIBLE AS A FOUNDATIONAL AUTHORITY AS WE SEEK TO LIVE THE CHRISTIAN LIFE.

What does this conviction mean? What are we trying to say? We call the Bible a *foundational* authority because we want to emphasize that engagement with the Bible is NOT optional for the Christian. The Bible is our foundation because it recounts our foundational story. It provides a history of God's saving acts. It puts us in touch with our roots. The Bible tells our story as a community. Faithful Christian living requires us to wrestle again and again with the biblical stories in order that we might hear God's Living Word for us. It is a *foundational* authority for us.

Why did we say "a" foundational authority rather that "the" foundational authority? We had much debate about this very point as a committee. We said "a" foundational authority for two reasons. First, we were aware, as were the writers of the Basis of Union, that while the Bible has an undeniably central role in our efforts to discern God's will for us in our time, it is not the only authority, precisely because it is always mediated in particular times and places. Second, in this document we have sought to make clear that Jesus as the Christ is central to our life as Christians. The source of authority in the Christian Church is Jesus as the Christ, and it is to that particular, historic self-revelation of God that we, as Christians, appeal. Some of us were concerned that to have said "the foundational authority" would have made the Bible, rather than Jesus as the Christ, the critical source of authority for us as Christians.[7]

GOD CALLS US TO ENGAGE THE BIBLE AS A CHURCH SEEKING GOD'S COMMUNITY WITH ALL PEOPLE, LIVING CREATURES, AND THE EARTH.

This conviction is surrounded by questions: "What is community?"; "Can I be faithful if I'm not in community?"; "Can all communities be of God?"; and "How can I be in community with all living creatures and with the earth?"

I believe I would be making a serious error if I tried to answer

---

7. General Council ultimately voted to delete the article "a" from this conviction.

these questions in isolation and that is what this conviction is about. It is essential to attempt to answer these questions within a framework of community. It is the committee's belief, based on the responses we heard from across Canada and indeed around the world, that to be faithful to God involves reading and working with the Bible "in community." The word of God is more readily discerned when we share with others our thoughts and experiences. Their wisdom and insights add to our own, sometimes challenging what we hold most dear.

There is risk in this conviction, the risk of being involved in community. Not all communities are life enhancing. Some can be soul destroying. There is also the risk that comes from sharing our most deeply held beliefs. When we bring them out of their personal dwelling place, they may be challenged, perhaps attacked, sometimes shattered, so that we must start again to build our way of being with God. Grief can be part of this work as we let go of old concepts and attempt to embrace new ones.

This conviction will most readily fit, I hope, in the church community. There our grief will be held and respected. There, also, our excitement and passion about God's Word can be shared without fear of ridicule or judgment. The challenge for The United Church of Canada is to build these communities where there are none and support them where they already exist. It is there our questions about living in harmony with all living creatures and indeed the earth can be held. It will be through our engagement with the Bible in community that God's shalom will begin to be reality.

GOD CALLS US TO ENGAGE THE BIBLE TO EXPERIENCE THE LIBERATING AND TRANSFORMING WORD OF GOD.

I remember something that Bishop Desmond Tutu said at the 33rd General Council when speaking of the apartheid system of South Africa. Along with the oppressive power of the white man to his country also came the Bible, the seed of Black liberation from white oppression. In the Bible the Black people heard the message that God created them in God's own image. It was a liberating and transforming message for their lives and made them intolerant of any political or religious message or system that would enslave them.

All through history, humankind has experienced the Bible as God's inspired source for liberation, both in a personal sense and in terms of the political, economic, and social conditions of life. Through the ages, Christians have come to the Bible with the expectation that God's living and active Word will meet us there with saving significance. And as Hebrews 4:12 reminds us, it can be a Word that is sharper than any two-edged sword, bringing to the world searing judgment as well as healing grace.

We know from experience, of course, that this doesn't always happen. The Bible has been used by people, principalities, and powers to support racist and/or sexist actions and behaviour. Women, children, and people of colour have suffered in their humanity because the Bible has been interpreted in ways that bring injustice to the earth.

Not everything that follows as a consequence of Bible engagement is liberating. That is why we have stressed in our document that the Bible's authority has a direct relationship to its application, and in that sense is a derived authority. We have also stressed that the Spirit of Christ must be the ultimate standard or criterion for Christians as to what is liberating and what is not in that application. Jesus Christ is the foundational authority for testing even our engagement with scripture. And we are driven back, again and again, in the light of the Spirit of Christ, to examine and question our

Bible engagement and/or interpretations as we seek to be faithful to God's life on earth.

GOD CALLS US TO ENGAGE THE BIBLE WITH AN AWARENESS OF OUR THEOLOGICAL, SOCIAL, AND CULTURAL ASSUMPTIONS.

The people in the Bible are people with particular backgrounds and beliefs, predilections and passions, social contexts and locations. Lois Wilson, our past Moderator, describes how different perspectives lead to different ways of telling biblical stories. For example, one day Lois sat with three aboriginal elders. They were discussing the story of Miriam and six other women who made Moses' leadership possible. Lois asked them, "How would you tell your children the story of Moses in the bulrushes?"

The elders replied, "There are three questions we would want to ask. First, how did Moses really feel about being adopted into another faith, another race, a foreign language group, a wealthy class? That's our story and our children's too. Second, how did he ever reclaim his Jewish roots, having been reared in a foreign culture? That's our story too. And finally, how did he become aware that he was called to leadership of his own people, rather than simply rising higher in the Egyptian hierarchy? That's our story also."

This encounter shows how the word of God is custom made; it is released in relation to our own particular needs for healing and forgiveness. To say that scripture must be interpreted contextually means to be open to and inclusive of the yearning of the whole creation for justice, freedom, and peace. Every interpretation is driven by interests shaped by our personal and social contexts. This is not wrong — it is simply fact. While we often begin with our own personal needs — with an awareness of our own conflicts, anxiety, guilt, frustration, alienation, loneliness, fear, as well as our thirst for real life — the context of biblical interpretation goes beyond our personal needs. While we are shaped by the theological, social, and cultural roots of our unique lives, these are also intertwined with other people's in pain and oppression, as well as in hope and in joy. When we are deeply in touch with our own pain and the suffering of others, and when we celebrate the gift of life, then the Bible's story of healing and liberation can be read with an appreciation for the differences we meet in it and in our lives. In short, becoming conscious of our assumptions helps us to be more faithful in our journey with God.

GOD CALLS US TO ENGAGE THE BIBLE WITH A SENSE OF SACRED MYSTERY AND IN DYNAMIC INTERACTION WITH HUMAN EXPERIENCE, UNDERSTANDING, AND HERITAGE.

This conviction takes seriously the Bible as a witness to the living God and does not replace the divine work and presence among us; the Bible lives with and interacts with other sources of God's revelation and authority for us. It points to a God who has been revealed to us; and yet one who remains mysterious and free, who is present and absent; belongs to us, yet is not our possession. We come before this God with wonder and awe, and we come, too, with our experience, understanding, and heritage. We engage the Bible as the people we are, not as actors. God continues to speak for and act in our lives and is not confined to the covers of the Bible. At the same time, we bring good, critical, and sound scholarship to the Bible because it enhances our hearing and response to its story. The Bible spoke for its own context and can speak to ours.

GOD CALLS US TO ENGAGE THE BIBLE TRUSTING GOD'S SPIRIT TO ENLIVEN OUR UNDERSTANDING AND TO EMPOWER OUR ACTING.

A necessary context for interpreting scripture then is a practical engagement for our understanding and acting; in other words, a transformation.

When we try to live the good news of God's incarnation, of human worth and dignity, of justice and love, we will be inspired by the Bible to live with thankful hearts. We will be empowered to live in solidarity with those who have been and are victimized, to live in commitment to those who work to free themselves, and to live in new sensitivity to the groaning of the whole creation.

In our ongoing interpretation, decisions, and actions, the liberating function of scripture will be present as we engage the Bible, trusting God's Spirit to breathe life into our understanding and to empower our actions.

920630